Be Selfish Eat Well Serve Many

Taking the Path to Your Happiest Life!

EVE ROSENBERG

© 2019 by Eve Rosenberg

ISBN: 978-1-7328506-2-0
Library of Congress Control Number: 2019914335
Printed in Delray Beach, Florida, USA by Eve Rosenberg

DISCLAIMER

This book is designed to provide general educational information about the subjects discussed and not to diagnose, treat, cure, or prevent any psychological, or emotional condition. It is not intended as a substitute for any diagnosis or treatment recommended by the reader's psychiatrist, psychologist or any other medical practitioner. Use of this book does not establish any doctor-patient relationship between the reader and the author or publisher.

The author does not assume and hereby disclaims any liability to any party for any loss, damage, or disruption caused by errors or omissions, whether such errors or omissions result from accident, negligence, or any other cause. No warranties or guarantees are expressed or implied by their choice of content for this volume, and there is no guarantee that these materials are suitable for the reader's particular purpose or situation. If you suspect you have a psychological or emotional problem, we urge you to seek help from the appropriate specialist. This book is not intended to be a substitute for the advice of a licensed physician or mental health provider.

Readers must rely on their own judgment about their circumstances and take full responsibility for all actions and decisions made because of reading this book and applying the recommended practices.

The author has made every effort to ensure the accuracy of the information within this book was correct at the time of publication. Any perceived slights of specific persons, peoples, or organizations are unintended. All names have been changed, and any reference to a specific story or instance is coincidental.

For more information, visit Eve Rosenberg at www.Lessonslearnedinlove. com or www.peoplepleasersreformacademy.com.

For my late parents, Livia and Leslie Rosenberg, and my twin sister, Judy Legare. You are my family and I love you always.

Acknowledgements

Everything we do in our lives to impact others happens, in large part, because of the way others have impacted us.

To my late parents, Livia and Leslie Rosenberg: You are my greatest teachers and soulmates. I miss you and live in honor of you each and every day of my life.

To my dear friend, Arlene Fleischman, aka, the redhead: Thank you for supporting me at a time in my life when no one else was. You're a confidence booster and I love you.

To the late Debbie Ford, my teacher, my mentor, and the woman who gave me my life back: a million times, thank you!

To my family and friends who continue to love and support me: I can't say thank you enough times to let you know how special you are in my life. It's because of you that I continue to forge ahead on my Happy Journey.

To my two fur babies, Tabitha and Priscilla: You encourage me to love in ways that fill me up and make life precious. I continue to learn and grow by watching you.

My dear editor, Lisbeth Tanz: I am blown away with your creativity and expertise to make things speak and sparkle. This book could not have happened without you.

To Diana M. Needham: You're a godsend! Without your support and expertise in publishing, I wouldn't have had the patience or tolerance to self-publish one book, let alone two and more to come! Thank you from the bottom of my heart.

To Sam Horn, The Intrigue Expert: Hiring you as my writing coach was the best thing I ever did in my life. It's because of you that the writer part of me keeps writing!

To my coach and dear friend, Mindy Schrager: No one knows my inner thoughts and tribulations like you do. Thank you for your support and allowing me the safe space to explore myself.

To you, my dear reader: Thank you for allowing me to inspire you. Your time is valuable, and I'm grateful for your attention. I hope my book delivers the peace and joy I intended for you.

Table of Contents

A Note to The Reader

You are Unique.

You may not think that the world needs you, but it does. For you are unique, like no one that has ever been before or will come after. No one can speak with your voice, say your piece, smile your smile, or shine your light. No one can take your place, for it is yours alone to fill. If you are not there to shine your light, who knows how many travelers will lose their way as they try to pass by your empty place in the darkness?

~ Unknown

Introduction

On my personal quest for happiness, I've discovered that anything we don't want to be will limit our chances to become that which we yearn so deeply to be. Happy. Peaceful. Safe. Loved.

Along with our strongest desires, there's a universal longing for the certainty that we're worthy, that we matter, and that we make a difference in the lives of others. No matter what it is that each of us does in this world, we will question our impact. Once we believe we're helping and inspiring the people around us, we prosper.

But because we avoid taking care of ourselves by not tending to our own needs and desires, we embody the "be there for others no matter what" guidance. We focus outside of ourselves to please others in the hopes that we'll attain that which we seek. All this does is make sure we move further and further away from the outcome we desire.

Even though all the evidence proves we're on the wrong track, we're exhausted, losing patience, and becoming overwhelmed and frustrated, we remain the diligent students we're encouraged to be and continue to pursue a path that's futile in terms of attaining love and happiness.

Why?

Because no matter what, there's nothing worse than being *Selfish!*

For years now, my mind has been at me at various times of the day: Waking me from a sound sleep in the middle of the night with nonstop chatter. *Write the book! Write the book already!*

And so, I agreed that giving in to this request was in my best interest as well as anyone else who desired to live a happier life. Hence, *Be Selfish, Eat Well, Serve Many* is a story that will have you rethink what being selfish is really about, why it's essential to integrate and embody this quality, and how it will bring you everything you want, while giving back in spades to the world. It will support you to recognize how making yourself your first priority has been the solution all along to attaining the life you've always wanted. Your happiest life—I wish this for you. Now and always.

CHAPTER 1

Monday Morning

The sun rose on another blustery, early spring day in New York City. Janice yawned and sat up in bed. It was another Monday; another week doing work she'd lost all passion for years ago. She got out of bed and looked out the window of her fourth-floor apartment in the Upper West Side of Manhattan. A plastic grocery bag floated by, and she sighed. She felt as aimless and unfocused as that bag looked being carried along by capricious winds.

She yawned again, put on her slippers, and shuffled out into the main room of her large, sunny apartment. She spotted Xander, her glossy-haired black gerbil, running on his wheel. "Getting an early start to the day, huh, Xander?" she asked as she put her face up to the glass of his enclosure.

Xander jumped off the wheel and ran to face her. He put his left paw on the glass, and Janice put the tip of her right index finger up to meet it. They'd been doing that since he first came to live with her. She felt a strong connection to Xander; she believed he understood her.

"Good morning, Xander. Where are your cage brothers?" she asked looking for the two younger gerbils, Russ and Gus. "Oh, I see they aren't too troubled by your running," she said after spotting them curled up, still sound asleep. She changed their water and put fresh food in their bowl. Xander followed her every move and jumped into the food bowl even before she'd put in down. She admonished him as she did every day, "Xander, leave some for your brothers." Xander wasn't listening.

After a quick shower, Janice puttered around in the kitchen. The first order of business was making pancakes, the gerbils' favorite treat. As she headed toward their gerbilarium with three tiny pancakes, Xander began to squeak excitedly. Russ and Gus, who were now awake, joined in harmony. After receiving their quarter-sized prize, each gerbil retreated to a safe space away from the others to nibble contentedly.

"You guys act like it's a delicacy. I'm amazed at how the simplest things make you happy."

She pondered that thought for a moment as her eyes roamed the room. She lived alone, except for the gerbils. Her apartment was beautifully furnished, nested in a sought-after building. Her bank accounts were full, and her retirement was set. She'd had her priorities and insisted on meeting them almost religiously. But her last relationship had ended five years ago. *Gosh. Five years. I wasn't even forty yet*, she thought dejectedly. *I still thought I had so much time. Joe wanted a simple life; I wanted security and no money worries. I wish I'd understood his vision then. But I sure get it now.*

The gerbils finished their treats and began to groom, which caught Janice's eye. She laughed. "I'm so glad I have you guys to keep me sane and make me laugh." Each stopped grooming at the sound of her voice and stood up expectantly. "Sorry, guys. Only one pancake per customer." She glanced over at Xander who was bigger and taller than the other two. He winked at her. Janice smiled and winked back.

Her gloomy thoughts banished, she set her sights on having a good Monday at work. She cleaned up the kitchen, applied the last of her makeup, and made sure her journal was in her briefcase before she put on her coat. As she closed the door to leave, she called out a cheery, "Bye, kiddos!"

CHAPTER 2

Corn

"Who ate all the corn... *Xander*," Russ said grumpily as he rummaged in the food bowl.

"So? You weren't up. You guys sleep the morning away. Early gerbil gets the corn, *Russ*," Xander replied.

"It's not fair, Xander," Gus said as he took up a position next to Russ in the bowl.

"Who said anything about fair? We're gerbils, guys. Eating is what we do," Xander reminded them.

"So? Gerbils can have rules," Gus insisted as he climbed out of the bowl. "I say, no eating all the corn in the morning!" He punctuated his edict by pointing at Xander.

Xander, unfazed, chuckled. "Fine. You can have your rule... for you guys. I'm not listening. I like corn. If you want to eat some of what She puts down, get up earlier."

Gus's nose turned pink, a sure sign he was angry. He stomped away to chew on a toilet paper roll.

After finding nothing exciting to eat, Russ climbed out of the bowl, too. "Why ya gotta be like that, Xander?" Russ pleaded. "We don't ask much. You're the king here," he added, standing on his hind-legs and spreading his arms wide.

Xander shook his head. "I'm no king, Russ. I was just here first, and I'm the oldest. I also like to get up early."

Russ persisted, "But Gus is right. It's not fair that you eat all the corn."

Xander looked at Russ and scratched his head. "You're telling me that it's not fair that you and Gus don't get to eat any corn. Am I right?"

Russ nodded.

"Then does that mean you think your life is unfair?"

Russ opened his mouth and then closed it. His brow wrinkled as he considered Xander's question.

"I guess so," he finally answered.

Xander nodded. "You're right. It isn't fair because that's how you *see* it."

"Wait, what?" Russ looked confused.

"We all see life from our own perspective, Russ. How we choose to interpret life is up to us. Our view is always right because that's what we see," Xander explained.

"So—I'm right?" Russ still looked confused.

Xander climbed out of the bowl and moved closer to Russ. "You feel like life's not fair because you don't get any corn in the morning, right?"

Russ nodded.

"You're right. It isn't fair that you *don't get* any corn in the morning. But here's the kicker—I think life is fair because I *get* all the corn...because I get up earlier."

Russ stammered, "I... I…"

"All I'm saying, Russ, is that we're both right because we see life from our perspective." Xander continued, "You're always correct in the way you see things. It just depends from where you're looking at them."

"Oh," said Russ quietly.

"How do you think you could get some corn for yourself?" Xander asked.

Russ cocked his head and looked at Xander. "By getting up earlier?"

"Yes!" Xander clapped him on the shoulder, and Russ winced a bit.

Russ cocked his head and pondered Xander's message. "So, you mean you'd share the corn with me?"

"Of course! I eat the corn because I can. I don't do it to be mean, but I'm not going to leave any if I'm the only one up to eat it. I love corn! I choose to get up earlier to enjoy the corn. I'm creating the experience I want to have. I don't need to ask permission from anyone to do that."

You and Gus choose to sleep later. And, because you choose to sleep later means you both miss out on eating the corn, and that's the experience you choose to have. Here's the thing, Russ. You're the *only one* who has control over your life, despite what Gus might say."

Russ looked surprised. "I do?"

"Of course, you do!" Xander said, nodding. "You have way more control over your experiences than you can imagine. All you have to do is decide to be the one in control."

Russ scratched his head. Xander was saying things he'd never considered before. Most of the time, he spent his days making Gus happy. It had never occurred to Russ that he could make himself happy. He looked over his shoulder where Gus was busily gnawing on a stick.

"Do you think Gus will believe that?" he asked Xander in a hushed voice.

Xander nodded. "Gus already knows it. He didn't hang out here with us, now did he? He just went away to do what he wanted. Since Gus has lived here, he's done exactly what he wanted when he wanted, regardless of what you wanted to do, right?"

Russ's eyes grew wide. "I never... I mean... he's so needy."

"Yes, he is. But I think he might use that to control you, Russ," Xander decided. "And you let him."

"Oh!" Russ's gerbil brain was blown. This was a whole new way of thinking for him.

"Gus isn't going to like it if I go do my own thing, is he?" Russ asked, nervously.

Xander shook his head. "No, he probably won't. But that doesn't mean you shouldn't do it."

Russ reached out his paw to grab the food bowl so he could steady himself. "Xander, I never would have thought of these things in a million years. It makes my brain hurt a little. And I wonder where else I'm letting Gus control me." He rubbed his head.

Xander placed his paw on Russ's shoulder. "I know this can be hard to take in. But know that being in control doesn't mean you need to be a jerk to Gus...or me to get what you want. We can talk about that another time. Now, let's go see if Gus is still mad."

CHAPTER 3

Saturday, Late Morning

Yuck. Janice rested her head against the window as she watched the torrential rain. A flash of lightning made her blink; the immediate thunder caused Gus to squeak. He'd always been afraid of storms.

She moved from the window and knelt in front of the cage. "It's okay, Gus. It can't get you."

Gus was having none of it and buried himself deep into the shavings. She noted that Russ and Xander were sleeping, blissfully unaware of the storm.

She sat on the couch and turned toward the window again. She craned her neck to look up at the sky. Nothing but dark, rain-soaked clouds as far as she could see. *Today's a bust.* Her thoughts were as gloomy as the clouds that crowded the sky. Her plan had been to spend the day shopping at her favorite boutiques, eating a leisurely lunch at that new bistro that's been getting good press, and taking in the sights and sounds of the city she loves. But now—rain. *Sigh.* She considered going anyway for a half second but decided that staying in was safer—and drier.

Still scowling at the rain, she went into the kitchen and filled the kettle with water and placed it on the burner. *Tea makes everything better.* Although it was still raining hard, the storm itself had quieted. The bright flashes of lightning and loud bursts of thunder had moved on. While she waited for the water to boil, she noticed that Gus had emerged from his hiding spot. She rummaged in the fridge and pulled out a bit of carrot for him.

"Here you go, Gus," she said as she lifted the cage lid. She patiently waited for him to take the carrot. He sniffed it suspiciously at first. Realizing it was something he liked, he snatched it from her fingers and ran away. She heard a quiet *munch, munch* as he hunched over his prize. He'd look up occasionally to make sure no one was sneaking up on him to steal it. "Gus, you are an interesting gerbil," she said as she replaced the cage lid. Just then, the kettle began its distinctive whistle as the water began to boil, and she headed back to make her tea.

Janice, now cup in hand, was still unsure of what to do. She placed her steaming cup on a coaster on the coffee table and plopped onto the couch. Then she stared at her overstuffed briefcase. *Oh, there it is: that pang of guilt for not working on my day off.* Work. It was a means to an end which was a substantial income. It was the path she'd chosen because she never wanted to worry about money, and her lengthy career success now ensured she'd have a safe, secure future.

As she looked out the window again, her thoughts drifted. She'd decided after college to maximize her extroverted personality by focusing on a sales career. She chuckled remembering her dad's prideful comment, "Janice could sell wood to a woodchuck...if woodchucks used money." *Dad always supported my decision even though he thought I'd work with him at his pet store. I just couldn't see myself staying in Syosset, Long Island my whole life! I know leaving was the right decision for me.* She looked away from the window and her eyes landed on her briefcase again. *I used to love my work. But it hasn't brought me joy in a long time.* She wondered when she'd lost control of her life, turning it over to work, work, work all the time. *Maybe it's time for me to retake control. I just have to figure out what that means.*

She closed her eyes for a moment. When she opened them, her gaze fell on the photograph of her parents they'd given her last December. *Gosh, they look so happy.* She smiled. She'd always admired her parents. *Mom and Dad took good care of us kids, but they sure also took good care of each other in how they honored themselves as individuals.* She turned her body so that she could lie down. With her head on a pillow, she allowed her thoughts to drift.

Growing up on Long Island had been a dream. Her parents' house was a relic, built in the late nineteenth century. The three-acre tract it sat on had provided so much room for adventure and fun. Janice smiled remembering how she and her friends, and occasionally her annoying younger sister and brother, had scaled old walls, explored the nearby woods, and spent hours pretending. The house was too big for her parents now, but Janice knew they kept it with the hopes there'd be grandchildren one day to play there.

Sorry, Mom and Dad, she thought sadly. With her sister in Paris pursuing an art career, and her brother working insane hours as a stockbroker, it seemed no one had time for a relationship, much less children. Janice wasn't sure how much her parents dwelled on their lack of "grand offspring." They had busy lives together and separately. *Mom had always been independent, even when raising the kids.* Janice smiled as she recalled the first time her mother declared her desire to take a vacation. "Lenny, I need a break. Let's have Mom watch the kids and you and I go somewhere." They didn't know twelve-year-old Janice was listening from the doorway. She could see how tired her mom looked and that the talk of getting away seemed to revive her.

"Ellie, I can't leave the store. You know that," had been her dad's reply.

Ellie had simply stared at Lenny for several seconds in silence. Without missing a beat she'd declared, "Fine. I'm going by myself then." And she did. *I think I learned how to take care of myself from Mom,* Janice thought as she sat up to take a drink of her tea. Her mom went on several trips by herself. Each time she came back, she seemed energized and happy. Eventually, she gave up taking trips and instead pursued her education, achieving a bachelor's degree in psychology and then a master's degree in social work by the time Janice was twenty. *Mom's a go-getter, that's for sure.*

Her thoughts turned to her dad. Lenny had had a successful sales career when he came home one day and announced he was quitting to buy a pet shop. Her parents rarely argued, but they did for days after this proclamation. Eventually, Ellie agreed, once she understood how burned out Lenny was. The constant travel hadn't been good for him. He was overweight, out of shape, and cranky most of the time. She agreed to this change, but only under one condition—that he start exercising and eating better. Lenny agreed.

Being a family man, Lenny insisted that their three kids come with them to the sales contract signing. "This is a big deal, Ellie. The kids should be part of it." Once the paperwork was done, they drove to their new store.

Janice reflexively wrinkled her nose as she remembered her first impression. *Yuck. This place sucks. It stinks, too. And where are the animals?* Dad explained that the place had been for sale for a while. The original owner had died, so the animals had been sold to other shops in nearby towns.

"But I guess nobody took the time to clean the cages after the animals were sold," he surmised, looking around.

Ellie ran a finger across the counter and looked at the dirty result. "It looks like we have a lot of work to do, Lenny."

While their parents discussed how to tackle the various projects, the kids explored. All the cages were empty, which had made Janice feel better. She hadn't realized how worried she was that someone might've been left behind. She remembered trying to look at the store through her father's eyes. *Gosh, the place was such a wreck. It's no wonder they got such a good deal on it.*

The Syosset Pet Emporium opened for business six months later. It had taken that long to clean it, paint it, redesign the floor plan, and find the right fish, mammals, and reptiles for the area. *Mom was such a good sport about everything. Talk about something taking over your life! I guess that's why she needed her trips. Two years of nonstop work on the shop was enough for her.* Janice made a mental note to ask her mother more about that time in her life.

The store was a magical place. Janice loved being there playing with the animals. She didn't even mind cage-cleaning duty. There was something about being in the space her parents had worked so hard to make theirs that made her happy. Her dad was happy, too. True to his word, he started an exercise program and ate the healthy meals that Ellie cooked for him without complaint. Even though he still worked long hours, his health improved, and his mood was joyous most of the time.

They both found what makes them happy, and that translated into everyone being happier. Janice pondered that thought. *Mom and Dad weren't afraid to go for what they wanted, even if it made things uncomfortable or unhappy for the other person for a while. They each took control to get what they needed. I know there's a lesson in there for me somewhere.*

She sat up again and walked over to her briefcase. She knelt in front of it and reached in. She rummaged around, finally finding her journal that had slid beneath her many client files.

With her journal in hand, she walked back to the couch. All those memories had stirred up the need to write. As she piled pillows together to make a cozy writing space, she thought about the creative writing class she'd recently taken where her journaling adventure had begun. Taking the class had been decided on a whim. Winter nights can be long, and she wanted something new to do. She'd found the class at the local university extension and had enrolled on the last day possible after thinking about it for weeks.

The instructor had insisted that journaling was the key to successful fiction writing. She'd found the creative writing process to be exciting and invigorating—so different from her job. But true to her contrarian nature, she wasn't really journaling in the way the instructor had explained. After attempting traditional journaling for a week, she wearied of writing only her thoughts, which tended to be boring and often circuitous. Instead, she'd developed her own method of journaling that was enormously satisfying, and which reinforced her love of the creative process. Writing filled her with joy and purpose, something she hadn't felt in a long time.

She snuggled into the pillows, moved her cup of tea closer, and started to write. She was soon lost in her thoughts as her pen scratched across the paper's surface. A squeaky noise caused her to look up from her writing. Xander had just stepped into the wheel. He started slowly, but quickly ramped up to a full run. "Where are you going, Xander?" she asked, not expecting an answer. She watched a moment longer and then returned to her writing. This time, she was smiling.

CHAPTER 4

Changes

Predictably, Russ's decision to be his own gerbil didn't sit well with Gus.

"Come on, let's go dig in the shavings, Russ," Gus demanded one morning after breakfast.

"Nah, I don't want to do that, Gus."

"But you love digging in the shavings!" Gus exclaimed.

"No, *you* like digging in the shavings, Gus. I like running on the wheel and climbing around," Russ replied.

Gus snorted and his nose twitched angrily. "Yes, you DO like digging in the shavings. You're just saying you don't to make me mad!"

It took all of Russ's willpower not to roll his eyes at Gus's drama. "Gus, it's okay if we don't always do the same things together. We can do our own things. You do your own things all the time." He put a paw on Gus's shoulder. Gus shook it off and stepped back.

Gus stood defiant. "Sometimes, I need to be by myself."

Russ's expression turned from concern to happiness. "Me, too!" He was happy that he and Gus had found common ground.

"No, you're different. You're not like me," Gus retorted.

At that moment, Xander wandered over, tired after running on the wheel. "What's going on here?"

"None of your business!" Gus snapped.

Russ turned to Xander. "You were right. Gus doesn't like that I want to do things on my own."

"Xander was right?! Right about what? Why are you talking about me? What—are you guys friends now? What about me, Russ?" Gus's expression shifted from anger to sadness and then back to anger. Russ moved next to Gus and rubbed his nose on Gus's to calm him down.

"I'm still here, Gus. I care about you. And yes, Xander and I are friends. You could be Xander's friend, too."

Gus stepped back. "It was you and me. We were adopted together. We're brothers! And now you're getting all self-centered and mean because you're friends with Xander." Gus turned away.

"Gus—" Russ began.

"Leave me alone. I'm going back to my spot," Gus said, grumpily.

"You mean *our* spot," Russ corrected.

"Not anymore," Gus answered over his shoulder.

Russ sat down, dejected. He looked at Xander and then back at Gus, who was making a big show of moving all the shavings around in the spot he used to share with Russ. Russ felt very alone. He didn't hear Xander move next to him.

"Hey."

Russ sighed. "Hey," he replied with no feeling.

"It's going to be okay, Russ," said Xander, as he sat down.

Russ shook his head. "I've never seen Gus so upset. I'm not sure it will be okay."

"He'll come around. It might take a while. Nobody likes change—especially when they feel like they're on the losing end like Gus does right now."

Russ looked over at Xander. "I hope you're right."

"You have every right to want to do your own thing. You have every right to say no when something doesn't feel right. You have every right to want things. You took a huge step today with your brother. That tells me that you want your freedom more than you fear his reaction, even if you don't like what he's said to you or how he's acting."

"I wish I felt better about it. It seems self-centered and mean for wanting to do other things." Confusion etched across Russ's face.

"Russ, Gus is going to say things to get you to go back to the way things were. Standing up for yourself is the only way to get the things you want. But trust me when I say this: You must take care of yourself first. Sometimes, though, that means others will judge you for behavior they don't agree with. And I'd wager that's what Gus is thinking right now. You're not doing what he wants. Remember what I said about seeing life from your point-of-view? Gus sees what you're doing from his vantage point. It looks mean to him, and that's how he's interpreting it," Xander explained.

He continued, "You have the right to your interpretation, Russ. And, there are times when being self-centered and mean is necessary to take care of ourselves. We don't have control over how other people think or feel. As nice as we are, sometimes others feel sad or angry about our choices. We must be true to ourselves. Just like when I eat all the corn. My intention is not to be mean or leave you guys without food. I'm just hungry and no one's around so I take advantage of it."

Xander paused. He noted that Russ appeared to be listening intently, so he continued, "Plus, you and Gus have much to learn from each other. You're a teacher for Gus as he's a teacher for you. We can all use a little more of what we see in others, and they can use a little more of what they see in us. For example, you can use more autonomy and assertiveness as reflected in Gus. He can use some compassion and consideration as you demonstrate for him."

Russ nodded thoughtfully. "I never thought of our relationship that way," he said at last. Then he sighed and looked back in Gus's direction. Gus was chomping on a peanut shell. When Russ caught his eye, Gus stopped, picked up his peanut, and scooted out of view.

Russ sighed again.

"I want to believe that, Xander." He paused. "It did feel good telling Gus I didn't want to play in the shavings."

Xander smiled. "See? You're getting the hang of what it feels like to stand your ground on your behalf!"

CHAPTER 5

Sunday, Late Afternoon

Janice stuffed her client files back into her briefcase. *I'm so glad that's finished. I wish Everett would hire more salespeople. It's too much for Nathan and me.* She shook her head thinking about all the Sundays she'd spent working instead of doing other things. She leaned back in her armchair and rubbed her temples trying to will away the headache that threatened.

Her cellphone buzzed. *Maybe that's Dad,* she thought, smiling. Her smile faded as she read the caller ID: Everett. *Why would my boss call me on a Sunday?* She felt a sense of dread. *This call can't be good.*

She answered the call, feigning cheerfulness, which quickly waned once she listened. She bolted upright in the chair and sat perched on the edge. Her brow furrowed as she focused on Everett's words as he rambled on.

At one point, her mouth dropped open in shock. Janice felt her cheeks flush. Her hand trembled as she reached for her glass of water on the coffee table. She put Everett on speakerphone and took a gulp of water with her eyes closed as Everett continued his soliloquy. She put the glass down gently, she'd thought, but instead it hit the wooden table with an audible thump.

Janice grabbed her phone and stood up abruptly. She began pacing from one end of the apartment to the other. The gerbils noticed this movement, and they began pacing too, although they didn't know why. They sensed she was very upset.

As she listened, Janice was struggling to keep her emotions in check and stay calm. Everett droned on and his voice filled the space around her. She shivered as she took him off speaker-phone and put the phone to her ear. His tone had turned angry. Startled, Janice opened her mouth in disbelief and waited for Everett to finish his rant. She rubbed her forehead. The headache she'd tried to avoid was waging an intense battle now behind her eyes. She steadied herself as the call was wind-ing down and opened her mouth to speak. But before she got the chance, the line went dead.

She stared dumbly at her phone and then closed her eyes as she took a few deep breaths. She opened her eyes and stared at her phone again, realizing the call had lasted barely five minutes. To Janice, it had felt like an eternity. She looked up and spotted the gerbils watching her.

In her mind, Janice replayed the monologue Everett recited and resumed her pacing. Ever-ett had fired Nathan, the only other salesperson, that morning. He'd repeated the pattern he'd set with Emily, another salesperson, six months ear-lier, when he'd fired her on a Saturday. *What's with Everett and weekend firings?* she wondered glumly.

Nathan was so good at his job. Emily was great at it, too. I thought Nathan and I were doing well in picking up the slack. Emily had some big, demanding clients, but we'd managed to allay their concerns about her abrupt departure and kept the business. But doing Emily's work meant Nathan and I had no more personal life.

I can't believe Everett was throwing around the idea of a raise for me to make up for the extra work—as if that would make me feel better! I don't need more money. I need a life! I feel like an indentured servant. This used to be such a great company to work for. Now, with Everett making these rash decisions, it feels out of control. I feel out of control.

She paused in front of the gerbilarium. "How can he expect me to do the work of two other people and mine, too? I already work six days a week. Does Everett want it to be seven?" she asked as she looked at the gerbils. Russ and Gus watched her for a few seconds more and then scurried away from the glass. Xander stayed. He cocked his head and stared at her. And then he winked. "Aw, Xander," Janice said as she sat down in front of the cage. She winked at him. "You really seem to care how I'm feeling." She was touched and felt her emotions shift from anger to sorrow. She put her head in her hands. *I had too much work to do before. What's my life going to be like now?* As Janice looked up again, Xander wandered away.

She sighed and slowly rose from the floor. *I put myself in this situation.* She sniffled and took a deep breath, willing the tears not to fall. *I've given away my power for too long. I've lost control of my life, and I don't want to live like this anymore. I can't rely on corporate America. I need to make my own way.* She felt her anger rise again and reflexively clenched her fists. But she couldn't discern who she was angry at: the others or herself.

She dropped onto the sofa and hugged her knees into her chest, staring at nothing as her thoughts swirled. Her breath grew ragged, and she angrily wiped away one tear, and then another until there were too many to brush away. Soon, the only sounds were her sobs and the squeak of the wheel as Xander ran at full speed.

CHAPTER 6

Pigeon Wisdom

Russ and Xander were playing a game of chase. Xander zipped up the ladder to the second story with Russ not far behind. They tussled in the shavings, oblivious to anything going on around them. When they stopped to catch their respective breaths, they heard a voice.

"Hi there!" said the voice.

Xander looked at Russ. "Did you just say, 'Hi there?'"

Russ nervously shook his head. The voice came again.

"I said, 'Hi there!'" It was more insistent this time.

The gerbils slowly turned around to see an eye looking at them through the open window.

Russ responded by squealing and dashing down the ladder.

Xander sucked in his breath and hunkered down. The eye disappeared to be replaced by odd looking feet. Then, the eye appeared again.

"Hi, I'm Mabel," the creature said.

"Hi, I'm Xander," he replied.

"So nice to meet you, Xander! What happened to your friend? He left so quickly."

Xander crept closer to the glass wall of his enclosure. "I think you scared him."

"Oh dear. I'm so sorry. I forget that I can seem scary," Mabel answered.

Xander cocked his head. "So, what are you?"

"I'm a pigeon."

"How'd you get up here?"

"I flew."

"Flew?" Xander was confused.

"With these," Mabel said as she spread her wings.

"Whoa! Those are cool! How do those work?"

Before Mabel could respond, Russ poked his head over the top of the ladder. "Xander, is it safe?"

Xander, laughing, said, "Yes, it's safe. Mabel is going to show me how her wings work. Come on up, Russ!"

Russ settled in behind Xander. After Xander introduced Mabel to Russ, he said, "Okay, Mabel. Show us your stuff."

Mabel spread her wings again and leapt off the ledge.

"Oh no!" Russ cried. "Did you see that? She fell off the edge!" He began wringing his paws nervously.

Xander held his breath, hoping Mabel was okay. A second later, she landed on the ledge.

"See? She's fine, Russ," Xander said soothingly.

"So, what did you think?" she asked after folding her wings at her sides.

"It was awesome!" Russ exclaimed. Both Xander and Mabel were amused at his response.

"But what *are* you?" Russ asked. "You don't look like me or Xander."

Mabel patiently explained, "I'm a pigeon. Pigeons are birds. Birds have wings, although not all of us can fly. I can fly, though. It's how I get around, Russ. I could walk like you do, but I wouldn't get very far. And, I'd probably get eaten by a stray cat." She shivered at that thought.

Xander piped up, "Thank you for the explanation, Mabel. It's very nice to meet you." He nudged Russ with his back foot.

"Yeah, it's nice to meet you, Mabel."

"Likewise, boys."

Xander edged closer to the glass. "I've lived here for a while now, and I've never seen a bird on this ledge. Why are you here?"

"Oh, that's easy. The ledge wasn't being lived on by another bird." Mabel laughed.

Russ, feeling bolder asked, "Where are you from?"

"Well, I was living in Central Park with a whole lot of other pigeons. I thought that was the best place for me to be. I mean, I was born there. But man, there was so much competition for food! One day, as I was flying around, I found a much smaller park near here that has lots of people feeding pigeons, too. Except, there aren't as many of us in that place. I decided that's where I want to spend my days. I started looking for a home closer to my new park. I found this ledge on my second day looking. I like that it comes with neighbors, especially since I left all my friends in Central Park."

Russ moved, so that he was sitting next to Xander. He seemed fascinated with Mabel's story. "You mean you moved just for you?"

"I did. It wasn't an easy decision, but it was the right one for me. But it wasn't right for my best friend. She couldn't bear the thought of leaving Central Park. I even showed her the new park— all the trees, the slower pace of life, the nice people who feed us every day, but she couldn't do it. She and many of my friends said that I was being thoughtless and inconsiderate by leaving." She shrugged her shoulders. "Sometimes you have to do what's right for you regardless of what others might say."

Russ looked at Xander and then at Mabel with wide eyes. "Weren't you afraid?"

"I'd be lying if I say I wasn't, Russ," Mabel admitted. "But I guess you could say my desire to have a different life won over the amount of fear I was feeling about striking out on my own. And while my friends were upset, I never apologized for wanting a better life for me," she added.

Russ looked thoughtful as he considered her words. "Have you visited your friends in Central Park since then?" he finally asked.

"I sure have! And you know what? They were so happy to see me! They missed me. And nobody's mad at me anymore, but even if they were, I made the right choice for me. I have no regrets about leaving."

Russ appeared to tear up a bit as he looked at Xander. "There's hope for me and Gus isn't there, Xander?"

Xander nodded. "Yes, I believe you and Gus will find your new normal and be buddies again."

Russ beamed. "Mabel, you have no idea how much your story has helped me today."

"Happy to oblige, Russ," she cooed.

The three friends spent the rest of the time chatting. Mabel told them about all kinds of things Xander and Russ could never have imagined.

As Xander and Russ climbed back to the lower level, Russ said, "I sure didn't know I could understand pigeon. Heck, I didn't know pigeons existed!" He chuckled. "I liked her story—you know—about moving here from Central Park, whatever that is."

Xander smiled. "Sometimes life serves up exactly what you need, doesn't it?"

Russ nodded. "Her story reminds me of the ones you tell me, Xander. You both make decisions that serve you despite what others might think. And, gosh, Mabel seems super happy. So do you," he added, pointing at Xander. "I just need to start taking charge of my decisions without feeling guilty about Gus," Russ added.

"Great awareness, Russ! Mabel just went for it, didn't she? You're right. Her experience mirrors what we've been talking about regarding you and Gus. Like Mabel, you have to decide if what you want is stronger than the fear of making Gus upset. You must believe that you're worth the effort. Only then will you be able to break free, which will make you a better brother. After all, when you're happy, you'll serve others—in this case, Gus, and me, more effectively. But it has to start with you."

Russ nodded again.

Xander added, "The best part, Russ, is that you have all the information you need now to change your life. You simply need to decide to do it."

CHAPTER 7

Friday Afternoon

Janice sat idly tapping her pen on her desk and staring out the window. Her mood was sour, and her thoughts were cloudy. *Everett's blown me off all week. At this point, I'm sure he thinks I'll just go along with the decision he's made to have only one salesperson for this whole, huge company.* She began tapping the pen harder as she frowned at her thoughts. *I don't think I've ever felt this unmotivated in a job.*

A soft rap on the door stopped her thought spiral. "Come in!" The door opened slowly and her assistant, Kelsey, poked her head in.

"Can we talk, Janice?"

"Of course, Kelsey. Come in," Janice answered as she gestured toward one of the chairs in front of her desk.

Kelsey stepped into the office and closed the door behind her. Janice's eyebrows went up in surprise as she watched her. As Kelsey settled in a chair, Janice sat in its companion, so they'd be face-to-face. She'd never liked what felt like the pomposity of a desk between herself and her visitors, except for Everett. She could never put enough space between the two of them.

"So, what's up?"

Kelsey looked out the window for a moment, and then at Janice. "I'm sure you've heard about the plans for the company," she began.

Janice looked surprised. "Plans? Other than firing Nathan, I haven't been told anything." *Maybe that's why Everett's been avoiding me*, she thought.

"Yeah, well, I wasn't sure I should tell you, and maybe it's scuttlebutt, but the word in the office is that Everett's out." What Kelsey said next shocked Janice. "And you're in."

Janice was stunned. "What? Who told you this?"

"Marilyn. She's certain it's happening because she typed up the board meeting notes."

"Do you mean Marilyn, the assistant to Doug, the CEO? *That* Marilyn?"

Kelsey nodded.

"Board meeting? They weren't supposed to meet until next week." Janice was confused.

"It was an emergency meeting. Apparently, Everett went too far in firing Nathan. He's hobbled the company's ability to meet its quarterly sales numbers. I think the word Marilyn used was 'rogue.'" Kelsey kept talking, but Janice wasn't listening. Her mind was racing.

Everett's out. Oh, I hope that's true. But me...in? I don't even think I want his job. All the paper-pushing and managing of people. If it's true, I'll need time to think about it. Janice became aware that Kelsey was staring at her.

"So, what do you think?" Kelsey asked.

Janice wasn't sure how to respond. "Think? Think about what?"

"That you could be the big cheese in the sales department! You'll be so great at the role! And Everett's office has that ah-mazing corner view—all those windows!" Kelsey gushed.

"Kelsey, I don't know that any of this is true. I can't think about something like that without some proof that it's happening!" she responded.

Just then, a sharp knock on the door startled them both. This time, Janice rose from her chair and opened the door.

"Doug! What a pleasant surprise!" Janice hoped she truly did sound surprised. As Doug entered, Kelsey nodded at him and Janice and made a hasty exit, closing the door behind her.

Doug sat in the chair Kelsey had just vacated and put his coffee cup on a coaster on Janice's desk. He glanced around the office. "This is a nice space. You have good taste in art."

Janice smiled. "Thanks. I like to look at things that make me happy—especially when I'm working."

Doug nodded and took a deep breath. "There are some changes happening here, Janice. There's no easy way to say this, but I just fired Everett. He's packing his office now and will be escorted out of the building as soon as he's finished."

Janice again feigned surprise. "Okay, but why?" she asked.

"I'm sure you can guess. Everett has crippled our ability to make our sales numbers by firing two key personnel in the past six months. Letting go of one wasn't so bad, but two? That was a rogue decision that wasn't cleared by anyone. We can't expect you to take up all the slack in sales. That's an impossible task."

Janice relaxed and let out a breath. At least someone agreed with her on Everett's poor decision-making skills. He was leading the company in a bad direction. "I can't say I'm surprised about Everett. I couldn't fathom why he was tearing the department apart," she said.

Doug frowned. "Everett said his decision was based on a cost-cutting measure." He shrugged. "I don't get it because that excuse doesn't make sense."

Janice grabbed her water glass and took a drink. "No, I didn't understand his reasoning, either," she responded as she put her glass down. "And I appreciate you coming to tell me this. After he let Nathan go, I... I wasn't sure how things would play out."

He caught the meaning in her words. "We can't lose you, too, Janice. Of the three salespeople, you always outshined the rest. Emily and Nathan were competent, but you have something extra that always turns even the most difficult prospects into clients."

"Thank you. I do work very hard. Thanks for acknowledging that."

"Here's the thing, though," he said as he tented his fingers. "We need to replace Everett and retool the position. I want our VP of sales to carry a client load, too. Everett was too far removed from client interaction, and I think this contributed to his poor decision making."

"That makes sense," Janice replied. "Do you have anyone in mind?" His answer would have shocked her if not for Kelsey's heads up.

"Yes. You," he said as he pointed at Janice.

"Me. Me?" Janice repeated. "Oh, Doug, I'm not—" Doug cut her off.

"Look, you're the perfect person for this role. You know the company and its products. You'll be able to build your own team—you could even ask Nathan and Emily to come back. They were good salespeople and didn't deserve to be sacked from what I can see." He leaned closer. "The position also comes with a sizable raise and, of course, Everett's office would be yours. You could buy more art for the larger walls." He smiled and sat back.

Janice thought he looked a little like the Cheshire cat in *Alice in Wonderland*. Then she chastised her thinking. *Doug's a good guy in a tough spot. His job could be on the line, too.* "Doug, I need to think about this. I'm grateful for everything you're saying. I'll admit it does feel good to be recognized for my efforts and experience by receiving this offer. I need to think about how it will affect me and my life, which I haven't had much of for many, many months now."

"I had a feeling you might say that. I get it," he responded. He glanced around her desk and grabbed a pad of paper and a pen. He scribbled something on the paper and then handed it to her while placing the pen back on her desk. "This is our offer. I told you it was sizable. It reflects the added responsibilities and your experience. Plus, it's far more than what Everett was making. Let's just say it's the company's way of showing you how much faith we have in your abilities to right this ship."

Janice stared at the number with wide eyes. She looked up at Doug and said, "This will make my decision a little harder... or easier, depending." As she heard the words come out of her mouth, a jolt of excitement surged through her body as she realized that money was no longer her number one motivator for creating a happy life. For the first time, she had faith that joy was attainable and within reach.

"Good," Doug continued. "I know you're the right person for the job. You would be very hard to replace," Doug said as he stood from his chair.

Janice stood up to face him. "Thank you. This conversation has certainly puffed up my ego a bit. I do need to think about your offer, though. I'd like to take the weekend to consider it."

"Well, I'd hoped our offer would have made you jump at it, but, sure, take the weekend to think about it," Doug replied. He fished in his pocket and pulled out his business card. He grabbed the pen from her desk again and scribbled on the back of the card.

"This is my cell number," he said as he handed her the card. "Call me if you'd like to ask any further questions, okay?"

Janice took the card and nodded. "I will."

She walked Doug to the door and opened it for him. "Thank you again."

Doug smiled and said, "We'll talk Monday, if not before. Have a good weekend, Janice."

After wishing him well, Janice closed the door and leaned against it. *I did not see this coming. I have a lot of thinking to do.* She glanced at her watch and decided now was a good time to pack up and leave. She made sure to grab the pad of paper Doug had written on. No sense letting that lie around all weekend.

She spoke briefly with Kelsey before heading home. This wasn't any ordinary weekend. It was one that would change all future weekends to come. She could only speculate how much.

CHAPTER 8

The Showdown

Xander awoke with a start. *What's all that racket?* he thought grumpily. He stretched and yawned as he left his sleeping box. He quickly discovered the cause of all the noise. Russ and Gus were standing nose to nose chattering at each other. While Xander was not happy that his nap had been interrupted, he was pleased to see the young gerbils finally addressing their issues.

"You never spend time with me anymore. It's all *Xander* now!" Gus yelled at Russ.

"Well, at least he treats me like an equal," Russ countered.

"What's that supposed to mean?" Gus said through clenched teeth.

"We talk about all kinds of things. He shares his thoughts and teaches me things. All you do is tell me to do things, Gus."

Gus's ears flattened against his head. His eyes flashed, and he gnashed his teeth.

As Xander watched, he wondered what Russ would do.

"Gus, you can be angry if you want, but that's on you. I'm not making you angry. You're mad because you can't control me anymore, and you like being in charge. I know that. But I'm a better gerbil for hanging with Xander. And I believe—" Gus cut him off.

"I don't care what you believe," he seethed. "You abandoned me!" Gus's demeanor changed suddenly, and he no longer looked angry but, instead, sad.

"I gave you space, Gus. As I was saying, I believe *we*," he gestured to Gus and then himself, "will be better brothers for each other."

Gus turned away from Russ. "I don't know if I believe you," he said at last.

Russ moved next to Gus and touched Gus's nose with his. "Of course, you can believe me, Gus." Russ began fumbling for the right words. Xander took that as his cue to step into the conversation.

"Gus, your brother is right; you can believe him."

"Why should I listen to you?" Gus demanded. "You took Russ away from me."

Russ interjected, "No, Gus. You pushed me away, remember? You told me to sleep somewhere else, and that you were going to do your own things...without me."

Gus frowned as he thought. "I guess I did do that. But I was mad that you and Xander were doing things together the way we used to do."

"Gus," Xander said, "Russ needed some time to develop his relationship with himself. He loves you more than you know."

Russ nodded. "I felt like everything we did was what you wanted to do, Gus. I almost never got to do what I wanted to do with you. Xander helped me understand that it's okay for me to *want* to do my own thing with you or not. And there are things I like to do now that I didn't know I liked to do—like run on the wheel. It's fun!"

"Didn't you like the things we did together?" Gus asked Russ.

"Yes, but not all the time. Sometimes I want to be the one suggesting an activity. And sometimes I want to be by myself. You've always handled yourself well alone, Gus. Xander didn't teach me that, you did."

Gus smiled. "I did?"

"Yes, you did."

"So..." Gus began, "what's something you want to do, Russ?"

"I'd like to take you upstairs to meet Mabel the pigeon," he replied.

"I don't go up there; you know that," said Gus.

Russ nodded. "I know you don't go up there because you're afraid. I remember. But I can help you not be afraid if you'll let me."

Russ turned to Xander. "Tell Gus how I've changed, Xander."

Xander smiled and sat next to Gus. "Russ has been a great student, Gus. He's far braver than you probably suspected, and he's gotten to know himself well. And that's really the key here, getting to know who you are. You, Gus, get a gold star for knowing yourself well already."

"I do?" Gus asked incredulous.

"You bet!" Xander said. "You already knew all the things you like and don't like to do. Russ was okay following along, but it didn't leave him much room to grow into his interests. But now, he's met Mabel," Xander explained and pointed upstairs, "learned the joy of the 'Wheel of Opportunity,' and has even gotten up early enough to get some of the prized corn."

Gus's eyes opened wide at the last point. "Corn? Early? Really?"

"Yes, corn," Xander answered. "Russ has grown into his own by being away from you. By knowing himself, he's able to embrace those gifts he has and share them with you. Russ took a chance with me and it's paid off for him. He can now express himself in his own way, even if it's not what you might expect."

Russ spoke up then. "Xander taught me that I needed to believe in myself to be the best me I can be. That was hard, but I can see now how you and I are alike, yet different—in good ways. I also learned that it's okay to want to be happy. I deserve that, too."

Gus was quiet. Russ put his paw on his shoulder. "There's one more thing, I learned, Gus."

Gus looked up at Russ. "What's that?"

"I learned that I'm special, and so are you."

Gus looked surprised. "I'm special?"

Russ nodded. "Yes, you are, I am, Xander is, Mabel is, The Nice Lady is . . ."

"But why?" Gus seemed confused.

"We all have special gifts and talents, Gus. You have yours, I have mine, Xander has his, and Mabel—I can't wait for you to see Mabel's special talent!"

Gus was silent again. He finally spoke in almost a whisper, "This is a lot to take in. I didn't know all these things. I'm sorry I got mad at you, Russ. But maybe it was a good thing after all." He rubbed his nose against Russ's. "I need some time to think about all you've both told me. I need to be by myself."

"Take all the time you need, Gus. I know we've told you a lot of new things," said Russ.

Xander and Russ watched Gus walk back to his sleeping spot and snuggle into the shavings.

Russ's brow furrowed. "Will he be okay, Xander?"

Xander rubbed his chin thoughtfully. "I'm sure of it. He's just gotten a crash course in being a gerbil. You've had several weeks to process this information. It's a lot to hear. Gus will come around when he's ready. The good part is that he listened. I predict you and he will be fast friends again in no time."

"I think you're right, Xander."

They walked toward the food bowl together. "Let's have a snack, shall we?" Xander offered. Russ was always up for a meal.

As they munched, Russ asked, "Why did you call the wheel the 'Wheel of Opportunity?'"

Xander wiggled his nose as he chewed. He swallowed and then said, "Some gerbils think the wheel is just a place to get exercise. It's so much more than that. When I'm on the wheel, my mind is free to roam to whatever thoughts I care to think. Just yesterday, I was wondering what it would be like to be Mabel, having wings instead of arms. I imagined what it would feel like to fly. I think I ran even faster then."

Russ was transfixed.

Xander continued, "It's not just imagining things, though. I'm free to consider all kinds of things that could be possible even though we live in this small space. I get some of my ideas from the picture box the woman who cares for us watches occasionally. I can't really see the images, but I can hear what's being said. I don't understand it all, but I know that there's a much bigger world out there than what we have here. Mabel also helps me think outside our cage. Running on the wheel and thinking about things is how I came to know the things you and I have talked about."

"I may never think about the wheel the same way," Russ said, wiping his mouth.

Xander smiled. "Most gerbils just run mindlessly on the wheel going around and around. Even though that's what you're doing, your mind is free to go wherever you want it to go to find new opportunities to learn, grow, and expand your horizons. But only if you run on the 'Wheel of Opportunity.'"

After they climbed out of the food bowl, Xander placed his paw on Russ's shoulder. "Russ, I've taught you everything you need to know. I'm so proud of how you've taken charge of your life and started putting your needs first. You've grown so much and now understand that taking care of yourself means you can better take care of others. You've been a wonderful student and an even better friend."

The two friends rubbed noses and Russ squeaked happily.

"Hey, guys?" Gus asked quietly as he walked up. Russ and Xander turned toward Gus. "I've been thinking about what you both said earlier. Russ, I'm not going to be anybody but who I am, so don't expect me to change. But I also see that you've changed. I need to get used to the 'New Russ,' especially because he's the brother I really need."

Russ's tail began swishing back and forth joyfully. The brothers rubbed noses and squeaked happily. Xander patted his belly and smiled. The brothers began a game of chase.

"Come play, Xander," Gus called.

Xander waved his paw and shook his head. "No, I'm good. I might run on the wheel."

"The 'Wheel of Opportunity,' Xander!" Russ called.

CHAPTER 9

Friday Evening

Janice was exhausted by the time she arrived home. She flipped on the light in her apartment and heard the gerbils busily playing. Xander was running in his wheel.

"Hi, boys!" she called, her weariness lifting.

After changing clothes and grabbing a light dinner, Janice sat on the couch looking at the number Doug had written on the pad of paper earlier. *I never envisioned a salary like that,* she thought. *I totally deserve it, especially given that Doug wants me to take on Everett's role and carry a client load. I wonder if I'd get commissions, too...*

She rubbed her hands over her face. "There's no number that can seduce me anymore. You can't put a price on happiness." She resettled on the couch and began thinking again. *I need to get clear on what I want from now on.* She flipped the page on the pad of paper and created two columns, one pro, one con, her usual way of working through decisions. Quickly, she threw the paper in the trash and went back to her stream-of-consciousness writing.

"Oh, wow," she said in a whisper. The decision was clear.

She looked at her watch. "Cool. Nine o'clock on a Friday night and I know what I'm going to say to Doug Monday morning!"

Feeling pleased with her decision—and for once not second guessing it—Janice walked over to the gerbilarium to see what the boys were up to. As she stood by the cage, she noticed something moving outside the window. It was the pigeon who lived on the ledge now—and it was looking at her! "I should pick up some birdseed," she said to the bird, even though she knew building management frowned on feeding birds from the apartments. The bird seemed to bob its head at the mention of food. Still bobbing its head, it walked the length of the ledge and disappeared out of sight. Janice leaned forward and saw it nestled into a corner. *I'll get food tomorrow*, she promised.

Janice reached in and brought Xander out. He immediately began to purr. That was one of the things he'd done when her dad had pointed him out to her in his pet store. 'He's a lover,' her dad had said. He sure was. Xander, happy to be out of the cage, crawled on Janice, inside her sleeves (which made her giggle), and around on the couch. He was speedy, so Janice had to keep a keen eye on him to avoid losing him in the apartment.

Eventually, Xander grew tired and curled up on her chest to rest. He was still purring. Janice closed her eyes and thought she could feel the magic of his purr seeping all the way into her heart. She gently petted him with a finger, and she felt him relax.

She whispered, "I've learned so much from you, and I'll always cherish these moments we have together, Xander." At the sound of his name, his purring grew louder again for a few seconds, and then slowed again as he drifted to sleep.

A little while later, Janice, holding Xander gently in her hands, placed him near his sleeping box. He woke up and blinked at her. She gave him a head scratch. He yawned and stretched. As she replaced the top of the cage, he walked to the glass and put his left paw on it. Janice knelt and put her right index fingertip on his paw through the glass. He winked. She winked back.

CHAPTER 10

Goodbye

Russ and Gus woke up at their normal time and were surprised to find corn in the food bowl. They climbed in and began to eat with abandon. They never had this much corn to eat!

Between bites, Russ asked, "I wonder where Xander is. It's not like him to sleep late."

Gus shrugged his shoulders. "I don't know, but I'm glad we got here first!"

After eating and drinking their fill, Russ suggested they find Xander. He was worried.

"You worry too much, Russ," Gus said. "I'm sure he's fine."

They went to Xander's sleeping box, but he wasn't there.

"Where could he be?" Russ asked, his brow furrowing.

Just then, they heard a loud tapping. Their eyes opened wide in surprise and fear because they'd never heard that sound before. It stopped, but then started again. They looked around the gerbilarium but didn't see anything that could be making the noise. Russ tilted his head.

"It's coming from upstairs," he said, pointing.

"Upstairs?" It was Gus's turn to look worried. "I don't go upstairs."

"I don't want to go by myself, Gus. I don't know what that sound is or what's making it. You have to come with me."

They discussed—then argued about Gus's fear of climbing.

Russ finally said in exasperation, "Gus, what if Xander's up there and he needs us? We owe him that. Without him, we might still not be talking to each other."

Gus sighed and slowly nodded his head. "Okay. I'll go."

Russ started up the ladder, turning his head to make sure Gus was following him. He was, albeit slowly. Rung by rung they climbed.

"How are you doing, Gus?"

"Okay, I guess," Gus replied.

The tapping continued. It was even louder now that they were near the top.

When Russ reached the top of the ladder, he couldn't see anything amiss. He stepped off the ladder onto the upper level. The tapping had stopped. Gus reached the top, too, and positioned himself next to Russ.

"The tapping stopped," Gus said.

"Yeah, I wonder why?" Russ responded.

Before they could say anything else, a shadow fell across them from the window. It was Mabel! She saw them and began tapping on the glass again, this time frantically. Russ and Gus walked over to her. She stopped tapping and seemed to be talking, but they couldn't hear what she was saying because the window was closed. She changed her position and began tapping again. Russ watched her and followed her beak to where it seemed to be pointing.

"Xander!" he cried.

Xander was lying on his side facing away from Russ and Gus. They rushed over to him.

"Oh, Xander, I was so worried," Russ said as he reached out to touch Xander. The moment he did, though, he stumbled backwards saying, "Aaah!"

Gus looked confused. "What's wrong, Russ?" He reached out to shake Xander, but Russ stopped him and pulled him back.

"I don't—" Gus started to say.

"He's... he's gone, Gus," Russ said quietly.

"Gone? He's right… oh." Gus sat down hard.

Russ sniffed the air and cautiously moved toward Xander's still body. He listened for breathing, but there wasn't anything to hear.

"What happened to him, Russ?" Gus cried.

Russ struggled to breathe. He shook his head and couldn't sound out any words. He staggered toward Gus and then leaned on him, inconsolable. Gus rubbed his back and said nothing. They didn't move for a long while.

Finally, Russ rubbed his face and sat up to look at Gus. "It's just you and me now, Gus." They snuggled together, their heads drooping.

Mabel watched them from outside, seeing their reactions to Xander's lifeless body. Her wings sagged, and she sank onto the ledge, her head resting on the window. Her eyes were closed.

Xander was gone.

CHAPTER 11

Monday, Early Morning

Janice padded out of her bedroom dressed in her bathrobe and rubbing a towel on her wet hair. Today was the day her life would change! She was making coffee and humming a song that had gotten stuck in her head when the gerbils caught her attention. Russ and Gus were rapidly pounding their back feet on the second level. She'd never seen them do that before.

She pulled off the cage top and began to say something when she spotted Xander. She sucked in her breath. Russ and Gus moved closer to the window. Janice didn't notice Mabel looking in from the ledge.

"Xander?" When he didn't move, she slowly reached in to touch him with her finger. She could feel the chill and stiffness of his body. She shook him gently, not wanting to believe what she was seeing and feeling. "Xander? Come on, sweetie. Wake up." She pulled back her hand and stared. Less than a minute before, she'd been so happy. Now, she felt as if all the air had been sucked out of the room. "Xander!" she cried. "No! Why?" Tears slid down her face. She looked at Russ and Gus. "I'm so sorry, guys. I'm so, so sorry." She collapsed on the floor; the sobs wracked her body.

What am I going to do without him? her mind screamed. She rocked back and forth, trying to get her emotions under control. She hadn't ever considered that one day he wouldn't be with her. Her mind drifted to their cuddling Friday night. *Was he sick? He seemed okay, happy even.* "Oh, Xander! How could you leave like this?" Janice's tears slowed, and she sat up. She had to go to work and face Doug. She wiped the remaining tears away and stood up. She grabbed a tissue and blew her nose. *What do I do with Xander? I can't leave him in the cage.*

She grabbed her phone and hit a number on speed dial. After three rings, her dad answered, "Hello, sweetheart!"

Janice thought she could hold it together, but she started crying again. "Da—ad!"

"Honey, what's wrong? Are you hurt?" She could feel his worry.

"Nah, no, I'm okay. It's Xander."

"Is he sick? What's wrong?"

"Dad, he's... he's dead," she managed to get out before a sob escaped her throat.

"Oh, no. I'm so sorry, Janice. I know how special he was to you."

Hearing her dad's voice helped Janice to feel a bit better. "I don't know what to do with him, Dad. I can't leave him in the cage while I'm at work. Poor Russ and Gus. They found him."

"Our pets never live long enough," Lenny said. "As for Xander, what time does your vet open this morning?"

"I think eight o'clock, but I'll need to check," she answered.

"Dr. Walters will take care of Xander. And, if you want, you could have him cremated."

Janice's eyes filled with tears. "I hadn't even thought of that. Thanks, Dad. I'll stop at Dr. Walter's before I go to work. I think I have a box I can put him in. This just sucks. He wasn't even sick—at least not that I could see."

"Sometimes our animals decide to leave before they get sick. It's like they feel their purpose is over or something. I've had a lot of customers tell me this," said Lenny.

Janice heard her dad say something to someone that was muffled. Then, she heard the extension at her parents' home picked up. "Janice?" her mom said.

"Hi, Mom."

"Janice, I'm so sorry about Xander. Is there anything I or we can do for you? I feel awful for you."

"Thanks, Mom. No, I have to go to work. Dad suggested I take Xander to the vet so that they can take care of him. I'm going there as soon as I get myself cleaned up again." She needed to get off the phone and attempt to look presentable.

"Alright, dear. We're here for you," her mom replied.

They said their goodbyes and Janice disconnected the call. Before she put down the phone, she checked the vet's hours. She was right; they opened at eight. She put down her phone and took in a deep breath. Then she retrieved a small box from her hall closet and lined it with tissues. Giving Xander a comfortable bed made her feel a bit better. She ripped off a paper towel and reached into the cage, holding it in her hand. She wrapped the towel around Xander and gently lifted him out of the cage. As she did this, she saw Russ and Gus watching from the first floor of the gerbilarium. Janice carefully tucked Xander into the box and put on the lid. She placed him by her briefcase and retreated to the bathroom to do damage control.

I have to put this all aside until after I talk to Doug. That conversation seems so unimportant now. Better to get it over with and move forward. After a quick shower, she moved quickly to get ready. She managed to finish faster than she'd anticipated, which left her time to talk with Russ and Gus.

She fetched a baby carrot from the fridge and cut it into two pieces. She felt a pang in her heart as she realized it would never be three pieces again. Russ and Gus eagerly accepted their treats and seemed no worse for the experience of finding Xander.

"You guys are amazing and so pragmatic," she whispered while she watched them eat. "I'm not sure I'll get over him as quickly as you do."

She glanced at the clock. Time to go.

"I'll see you two tonight, okay? Bye, guys," she said sadly.

Janice headed out the door with her briefcase hanging from her shoulder. Her left hand firmly gripped Xander's box.

CHAPTER 12

Memories

Fall was now in full swing in Manhattan. The trees outside the apartment had turned a coppery gold and a bit more of a chill was in the air on some days. Thankfully, this day wasn't one of them, and She had cracked the window a bit to let in the fresh air.

Mabel, who had informed the gerbils that she'd be wintering elsewhere, was chatting amiably with the brothers. The subject, as it seemed almost always, was Xander.

"Do you remember when you and Xander met me the first time?" Mabel asked Russ.

"I sure do. We were both so surprised at seeing you on the ledge." He smiled at the memory. "Xander handled his surprise better than I did. I couldn't believe anything could soar through the air, although, I never really thought about it before I met you," Russ added.

"Russ gave me a heads up, which I appreciated," Gus interjected. "He already told me that you had wings for arms, although I had no idea what that meant exactly. When he told me that you could jump off the ledge and live..." Gus put his paws on his head and acted as if it exploded.

Mabel laughed. Then she sighed and looked a bit sad. "Xander was one-of-a-kind, that's for sure. I mean no disrespect to you two, but Xander was special."

Russ agreed. "Yes, he was." Russ sniffled as he often did when he thought of Xander. "I learned so much from him," he said at last.

"Me, too, although mainly through you, Russ," Gus said.

"I think we might all be better off because of knowing him," Russ said. "I was wondering last night if I could remember everything that he taught me and you, Gus. Want to try?"

"Sure. You have a lot more to remember than I do."

"That's the truth!" Russ exclaimed.

And so, as the brothers recounted the lessons Xander had taught them, Mabel listened patiently and occasionally joined in with commentary.

Remembering each lesson made Russ and Gus smile. When Russ mentioned the "Wheel of Opportunity," Mabel said, "What's that?"

Russ explained it just as Xander had. Mabel looked thoughtful. "Well, I don't have a wheel, but I might try thinking like that when I'm flying," she decided.

"It's life changing, Mabel. Gus and I both do it. We've built new things to play with because of what we imagined on the wheel. I'm not sure what The Nice Lady thinks we're doing, but she leaves our projects alone when our home is cleaned each week.

"Maybe I'll come up with a better way to build a nest!" Mabel said, smiling. "We pigeons are terrible nest builders. We have no imagination."

The three friends continued talking until well into the afternoon. Life was different without Xander in it. But they agreed that they had all grown because they'd known him.

"I miss Xander each and every day." Russ added, as sadness covered his face. "Why'd he have to die?"

As Russ' eyes begged for comfort, Mabel shot a compassionate look in his direction. "We will all die one day." She said softly. "When those we love leave us, we get to value our lives more. We don't have as much time as we think we do."

Russ nodded as he rubbed his chin. "Now that's a thought to ponder. I think I'll take a spin on the wheel."

"Hey, I'm next in line," Gus said as Russ moved toward the ladder.

Mabel cooed and then called out as she prepared to take flight, "Time to live your best life!"

CHAPTER 13

Sunday Morning, Six Months Later

Janice loved sitting in her parents' kitchen and drinking coffee with them. Despite having moved away when she was eighteen, it still felt like home. She smiled as her dad recounted his latest golf story. He and her mom had taken up golf together in their late sixties. Janice still couldn't fathom why, but they seemed to have a fun time of it and were happy with their hobby. She was glad they were getting exercise.

"It was so embarrassing, Janice. I hit the ball, but I shanked it. That means instead of hitting the ball with the fat part of the clubface, I hit it with the part that's by the shaft," Lenny explained. He started to belly laugh. "It was hilarious! I've never seen a ball go at such a crazy angle before!" He moved his arm to show the ball's trajectory. Then he laughed again.

Janice watched with amusement.

Ellie shook her head. "Your father's a maniac on the local course. I'm surprised we haven't been banned from playing there yet."

"I don't think I'd want Dad as a golf partner," Janice added, laughing.

As the laughter died down, Ellie asked, "So how's retirement treating you, Janice? You seem more relaxed and happier than I've seen you in a long time."

Lenny nodding in agreement.

"It's still weird to think I don't have to work again unless I want to. I *am* more relaxed and happier than I have been in years. Once I got home after telling Doug that not only wasn't I taking Everett's job, but I was also leaving the company, I just physically and emotionally fell apart. I didn't realize how much angst, worry, and stress I was carrying until it was all gone. Even though I had another month to go at the company, it was all cleanup stuff. He hired Emily and Nathan again, so all I had to do was transfer clients, and I was free. But that whole month was still torture because I'd come home to no Xander. I *still* look for him.

Ellie and Lenny looked at Janice sympathetically.

"I haven't been just sitting around doing nothing since my time ended at the company, though." She leaned down and pulled two books from the tote bag she'd brought along.

"What's this?" Ellie asked as Janice handed her a book.

"It's my new book," she explained.

"Is that Xander on the cover?" her dad asked.

"Yes, it is. He was my muse as I worked my way through my creative writing class and afterwards. I made up stories and gave each of the gerbils a voice. Xander, it turns out, was a very wise gerbil. All my writing was done pretty much in a stream-of-consciousness way. When I reread what I wrote, I realized that my Xander character was saying exactly what I needed to hear for myself."

Ellie gushed, "I'm so proud of you! The way you've written these stories, even children could read this book and learn from it."

"Honey, would you be willing to let me put a few in the pet store? I bet some of the folks who come in would be interested in it," Lenny said.

Janice grinned. "I was kind of hoping you'd say that, Dad. I brought ten with me."

"That's my girl!" Lenny said, laughing again. "Why don't we arrange a book signing event? Sooner than later would be good," he added.

"That would be awesome. I can get more books printed. But why did you say, 'sooner than later?'"

Ellie and Lenny each shot a glance at the other.

Janice stared at her parents. "Wait a minute. I know that look. Come on, tell me." She leaned back in her chair and took a sip of her coffee as she waited for an answer. Lenny blurted out the news.

"Janice, we're going to sell the store."

Janice nearly spit out her coffee. "What?!" Her cup hit the table with a thud splashing the brown liquid across the surface.

Ellie jumped up to grab a towel. "Janice, you can't be surprised," she said as she mopped up the mess. "We're not exactly young anymore."

Janice sat with her mouth open. The store had always been a refuge for her. It's where Xander had come from—and the boys, Russ and Gus. For a moment, she felt numb. Her brain couldn't grasp that she'd no longer be able to visit the various animals and fish her father so lovingly attended to.

"I guess I never thought about you selling it," Janice said.

"My dear," her mom said soothingly, "We're at a point in our lives where we want less responsibility. The store requires a lot from your father, even with his terrific staff in place. It's time for us to step back and enjoy our retirement years."

Lenny sat silent. Janice looked over at him and could see he wasn't totally on board with the idea. *The pet shop has been his life; it's his legacy,* she thought.

"Do you have a buyer yet?"

Lenny shook his head. "We've had it up for sale for about six months. We've had some nibbles, but nothing firm."

"Wait. You've had it for sale all this time and you didn't tell me? I'm not sure whether to be mad or hurt!" Janice exclaimed.

"Now, Janice," Lenny began, "You've gone through a lot. Losing Xander, leaving your job, learning how to not be a workaholic, figuring out what's next for you. We didn't want to add to your already full plate. Besides, it's just a store."

"Dad, it's *your* store. It's *your* legacy. But I accept your apology. You're right; I have had a lot on my plate since Xander died." She stared into her coffee cup. Looking at her dad, she asked, "Can you tell me what other reason pushed you to think of selling? I mean, I hear what Mom's saying, but..." Her voice trailed off.

"There's a big box pet store being built two towns over. I have a feeling that could hurt our business. So, it's a good time to let it go." His eyes wandered over to Ellie who was nodding her head.

Janice wasn't convinced. Her dad looked more sad than excited. "But what about all the families who've been your customers? What do they say?"

Lenny shook his head. "Nobody knows except you, your mother, the real estate broker, and me."

"Has business gone down?" she prodded.

He shook his head again. "Business is really strong, actually. That means now is the right time to sell!"

Janice thought he sounded like he was trying to convince himself of that fact. "Dad, you've beaten back the competition before. A big part of the reason the store is successful is *you*. It's not just your knowledge of everything that has to do with having a pet, it's your kindness, generosity, and sense of humor that bring people in and keep them coming back."

Lenny's lip quivered, and he looked away. "Thank you, Janice," was all he could say.

"We've talked about this for months, Janice," her mother interjected. "We also didn't tell you because we knew you'd be upset. Of the three kids, you've always been the one the most tied to the shop."

Janice nodded, lowered her head, and stared at her coffee again. After a moment she asked, "Could we visit the shop?" She turned her head to look pointedly at her dad.

He glanced at Ellie and then nodded. "Sure. It's closed today; we'll have it all to ourselves."

She looked at Ellie. "Don't you want to come, too?"

Ellie shook her head. "This is between you and your father. Besides, there's a new author speaking at the bookstore at two o'clock this afternoon that I'd like to meet."

Ellie stood and walked over to Janice. They hugged as Ellie said, "I'm so glad you came to visit. You should do this more often!" Ellie walked them to the front door and watched them get into

Janice's car. She waved goodbye as Janice backed her car out of the driveway.

When they arrived at the store, Janice watched her father unlock the weathered door to the pet shop. He stepped back and gestured, "After you!"

She grabbed the knob of the wooden door. The bell her father had attached on the inside ages ago tinkled cheerfully as she pushed the door open. Before she even stepped in, the sights and smells instantly transported her back to her childhood. She paused and closed her eyes. *I could be twelve again.* She felt a hand on her back. "Janice? Janice, are you okay?"

She nodded and walked into the store. Lenny turned off the alarm and flicked on the lights. The aquariums bubbled and gurgled. The gerbils and hamsters were all mostly sleeping. A few were running in their wheels or eating. She chuckled as she watched a hamster stuff his cheeks full of bounty, run a few inches away, and push it out into a messy pile. She tapped gently on the glass, but he was too busy with his loot to consider where that noise was coming from.

She noticed that some of the wall hangings and posters had changed and that the counter base had been painted a bright, deep blue. She pointed at it and nodded approvingly at Lenny.

"Yeah, we couldn't keep the white paint clean. Now, it could be dirty, but who knows?" he chuckled.

"We updated all the tanks and cages over the years." He pointed to changes they'd made that he thought she might not have noticed on other visits. Janice nodded thoughtfully.

The place is spotless. It seemed everything had a place, and everything was in its place.

"I have a great team. They keep me on my toes most of the time," her dad explained.

"Could one of them buy the shop?" Janice asked.

He shook his head. "None of them have the capital to buy. I know they're worried that we'll just close it without selling. This is our retirement. I'm not doing that!"

Janice prodded gently about sales. Lenny sat down at his desk and typed on the keyboard for his computer. In seconds, the accounting software launched. "Here, you can see for yourself." Janice leaned in and read the screen. She was surprised at how strong the business was. She asked a few questions to probe further and learned just how successful the shop continued to be.

"Dad, you've always been a masterful marketer, and you love people and animals. Like I said at home, you're why the store is doing so well." This time, Lenny waved away her compliment.

"I hired well. Plus, your mother is a big help around here. It's a collaborative effort."

"But you have some misgivings about selling, don't you?" she asked as she sat in the worn chair by his desk.

Lenny leaned back in his chair. It squeaked in protest. "Yes, I do. But your mother wants to travel and have fewer expenses. And, she's right. I'm not getting any younger. I keep hoping someone will walk in one day and say their dream has always been to own a pet shop." He looked at her. "It hasn't happened yet."

She was listening, but also musing. *What if—?*

Just then, her phone buzzed. She picked it up and looked at the screen. A telemarketer. She was about to decline the call and then thought better of it. "Dad, I need to take this call." Lenny nodded and went back to his computer.

As she strode toward the door, she declined the call and then put the phone up to her ear and said, "Hey, Nathan!" The bell on the door tinkled to signal her departure. Once outside, she took in a deep breath and shoved her phone into her back pocket. *Easy, Janice.* She walked for a block or so. She stopped in front of the local bank and leaned against the cool brick. Her emotions were swirling, and her throat felt tight. She inhaled deeply again and exhaled with a ragged breath. *What's going on here? Why am I so emotional? It's just a store.* But she knew it meant more than that.

As Lenny had talked, she'd gotten that familiar feeling right around her heart. She couldn't explain it. But it always came about when she knew she was onto something positive. She'd often had this feeling at work when she made a new sale. She'd had the same feeling after she'd decided it was time to leave. She'd also had the feeling when she saw Xander for the first time—and almost every time after that. The feeling was like a piece of candy made from excitement, coated with knowing, and sealed with positivity. She shook her head and smiled. *I'm so weird.*

She looked up and down the street. There were so many memories here. She slid down the wall until she was almost sitting and mulled the idea that had announced itself in her head a few moments before. *Am I really thinking about buying the shop? Could I do it? I have more than enough money to live on for the rest of my life. But I'd have to move out of Manhattan. Am I ready to leave the big city?* As soon as she asked that last question, she already knew the answer. She loved Manhattan, but she hardly ever did anything in the city anymore. It had stopped feeling special because she was immersed in it all the time.

Would Dad stick around to help me? I have a hunch he would. Mom would get to travel, and Dad would get to keep running the store—part-time. That wonderful feeling in her chest was back. She looked at her watch. Ten minutes had passed. *I need to get back before Dad sends a posse out to look for me.* She retraced her steps to the shop, mulling over the opportunity. When she reached the storefront, she looked up at the sign and smiled. *It's a lovely idea, but can I make this decision in ten minutes?* Then it hit her. "*The Wheel of Opportunity!*" *I've spent the last six months clearing my head and seeking new experiences—new opportunities!*

She pushed open the door and heard the bell jingle. She was surrounded by the familiar smells and sounds, and the sight of her dad behind the counter. *This is my "Wheel of Opportunity" she thought.* Her heart confirmed it. *I couldn't have dreamed of doing this if it wasn't for you, Xander. Because of your lessons, I've taken care of myself. Now I can see all that life has to offer and feel how much love I have to give. Thank you, Xander. Thank you for everything.*

As she closed the door, Lenny looked up from his computer and smiled. She walked toward him and stopped in the middle of the store. Striking a pose with her hands on her hips, Janice took another look around as if assessing the place. Lenny cocked his head, curious as to what she was doing. After scanning the room, she locked eyes with him and smiled. Spreading her arms wide she declared, "Since I was twelve, I dreamed of owning a pet store one day. Today, I'd like to make that dream come true. I'd like to buy your shop, Dad."

And in that instant, Janice had renewed faith that things were looking up. "I'm on the path to my happiest life," she whispered and then let out an audible laugh once she heard the harmony of squeaking coming from the gerbilarium in the back of the shop.

About the Author

Eve Rosenberg is an Integrative Life Coach and the author of *Your Happy Life Realized—How to Stop Putting Others First and Yourself Last, NOW!*

Eve compassionately supports others to step into their lives with both feet and create relationships that are joyful and intimate with themselves and others.

Born to Holocaust survivors to save their unhappy marriage, Eve has experienced trauma and drama in her life. As an avid People Pleaser for decades, she understands how this destructive behavior has wreaked havoc in her relationships. Chasing love through the opinions and accolades of others, Eve knows what it's like to feel lonely, unworthy, and lost. She also knows with certainty that despite what we have lived through, there is correction and renewal available whenever we're ready to claim it.

"Everything that has taken me to today has been for a reason. Therefore, I love yesterday, embrace today, and cherish tomorrow."

Along with being impeccably trained as a Master Integrative Coach by the late Debbie Ford and the Ford Institute for Transformational Training, Eve holds a Bachelor of Arts degree in Sociology/Psychology, a certification as a Holistic Health and Wellness Counselor, and has a vast employment history in corporate America. Eve lives in sunny Florida with her two dogs, Tabitha and Priscilla.